Two For Tennis

By **Amanda Brandon**

Illustrated by
Carissa Harris

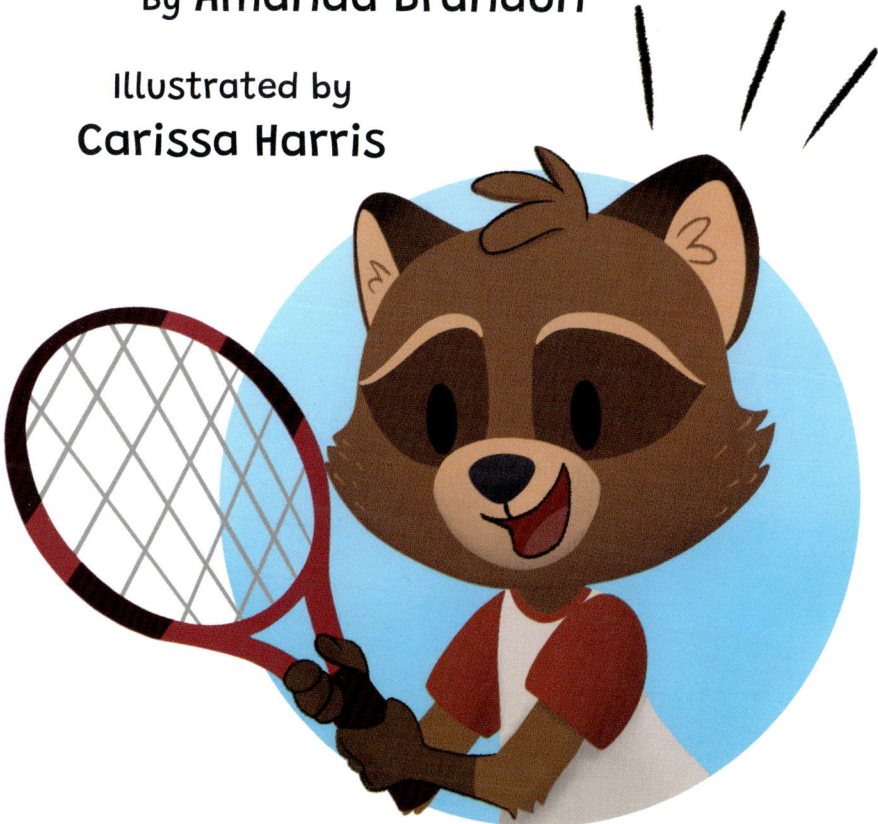

Ron wanted to play tennis.

DUDLEY PUBLIC LIBRARIES

The loan of this book may be renewed if not required by other
readers, by contacting the library from which it was borrowed.

CP/494

'Two For Tennis'
An original concept by Amanda Brandon
© Amanda Brandon 2023

Illustrated by Carissa Harris

Published by MAVERICK ARTS PUBLISHING LTD
Studio 11, City Business Centre, 6 Brighton Road,
Horsham, West Sussex, RH13 5BB
© Maverick Arts Publishing Limited February 2023
+44 (0)1403 256941

A CIP catalogue record for this book is available at the British Library.

ISBN 978-1-84886-936

Maverick
publishing
www.maverickbooks.co.uk

Blue

This book is rated as: Blue Band (Guided Reading)
It follows the requirements for Phase 4 phonics.
Most words are decodable, and any non-decodable words are familiar,
supported by the context and/or represented in the artwork.

"You need two for tennis," Mum said.

Ron spotted Fran and Sid.

"Will you play tennis with me?"

he said.

Sid said, "The ball is too quick."

Fran said, "The net is too high."

10

Ron huffed.

It will have to be just me!

Thud! Thud! Thud!

Ren looked over.

She said, "Can I play?
Tennis for two is better."

"Yes, you can play!"

said Ron.

Ren got the net.

Ren hit the ball to Ron.

Ron had a go. He flipped it back.

Ren jumped to get it.

Ren hit the ball.

It zoomed up high.

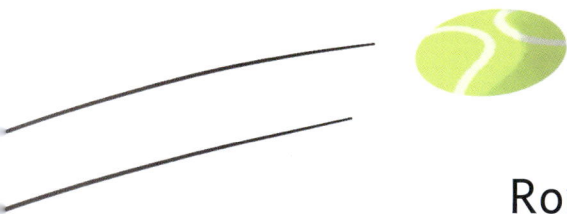

Ron hit it back.

Ren ran... but the ball was too quick for her.

Ron was the winner.

"Let's play again," Ren said.

"I want to be a tennis champ."

"Me too!" Ron said.

"And champs need...

...two for tennis!"

Quiz

1. Who finds the ball too quick?
a) Ron
b) Sid
c) Fran

2. Who finds the net too high?
a) Fran
b) Ron
c) Ren

3. Why was Ron in a huff?
a) He did not win
b) He did not have a net
c) He did not have two for tennis

4. Who wants to play with Ron?

a) Ron's mum

b) Ren

c) Tom

5. Who wins the match?

a) Fran

b) Ren

c) Ron

Pink
Red
Yellow
Blue
Green
Orange
Turquoise
Purple
Gold
White

Book Bands for Guided Reading

The Institute of Education book banding system is a scale of colours that reflects the various levels of reading difficulty. The bands are assigned by taking into account the content, the language style, the layout and phonics. Word, phrase and sentence level work is also taken into consideration.

Maverick Early Readers are a bright, attractive range of books covering the pink to white bands. All of these books have been book banded for guided reading to the industry standard and edited by a leading educational consultant.

Cool Duck and Lots of Hats
By Elizabeth Dale

Catch It, Jess! and Cat Nap
By Katie Dale
Illustrated by Kasia Dudziuk

The Space Race
By Jenny Jinks

Pirates Don't Drive Diggers
by Alex English, Illustrated by Duncan Beedie

A Right Royal Mess

To view the whole Maverick Readers scheme, visit our website at
www.maverickearlyreaders.com

Or scan the QR code above to view our scheme instantly!

Quiz Answers: 1b, 2a, 3c, 4b, 5c